THE TRIUMPH OF

M000222691

The Triumph of Poverty

POETRY INSPIRED BY THE WORK

OF

NICOLE EISENMAN

OFF THE PARK PRESS   NEW YORK, NEW YORK 2012

The Triumph of Poverty, copyright 2012 by
Off The Park Press. All rights reserved.

Cover image: The Triumph of Poverty, 2009
Oil on canvas by Nicole Eisenman,
(American, born 1965)
Painting, 65 x 82 inches
Courtesy of the artist and
Leo Koenig Inc., New York, New York

Book design by Shari DeGraw

To contact the press, please write

OFF THE PARK PRESS
73 FIFTH AVENUE, 8B
NEW YORK, NEW YORK 10003

ISBN 978-0-9791495-4-2

Off The Park Press books
are distributed by SPD

Small Press Distribution
1341 Seventh Street
Berkeley, California 94710
1-800-869-7553
orders@spdbooks.org   www.spdbooks.org

Printed on acid-free paper in the United States of America.

CONTENTS

JOHN YAU

INTRODUCTION

The Triumph of Poverty is the third volume in an ongoing series of anthologies of poetry devoted to the work of a single artist. For this volume we chose a painting by Nicole Eisenman. The first anthology was New Smoke (2009), which took the paintings of Neo Rauch as the starting point. In the second volume, we decided to write poems in response to Viva la Difference, an outrageous painting by Peter Saul. The fact that the painting was so over-the-top and was considered by many to be politically incorrect was very much part of the process. Some of the people we invited to contribute to the anthology, Viva la Difference (2010), ended up turning us down, because they felt the painting did not lend itself to being transformed into a poem. It is this kind of resistance that interested us. And who are we? A group of eight poets that has been meeting regularly for years to talk about poems, poetry, and anything else that crosses our minds.

The choice of Nicole Eisenman's painting was unanimous. There were no alternative candidates. We all loved it and thought it would be a challenge to write a poem about. We invited a number of poets, all of whom also got excited by the work and the prospect of writing about it. When we made the choice, it did not occur to us that the anthology would be published in an election year, amidst social uprisings and Occupy Wall Street. It was the painting that moved us to write these poems. We wanted to honor Nicole Eisenman's work as well as write something that conveys how deeply it spoke to our imagination.

KOSTOS ANAGNOPOULOS

NOWHERESVILLE

Too bad we don't live in a storybook
Where there's hope
You're too young to be in a poem
You never thought you'd leave a mark
And now you have
Streets and streams
Even battery powered ones
Ripple through everything
Maybe flag down some help
This is actually somewhere
Your first step
Down the grassy stairs
Into stationary vehicles
Distilling long distance
Wait here by the finger pointer
Study this rock, I'll be right back
The pronouncement of your so-called thing
Prevents us from recognizing the most important
    characteristics
Of our persona from the inside out
But you can't get inside a rock
Or take a rock to lunch
Well, you could...

Let's finish the other story first
The chant levels
Then call for help
Enough already with statements
Keep your balance
You don't need paper
Just tell us what's in there
Then go on ahead

GALE BATCHELDER

I SUSPECT YOUR CRAYONS

Someone left the patched love-doll in the driver's seat.

They are all wearing the one-eye profile except Oliver and The Baby.

The blind man in the blue cloak doesn't count because he's already lost his matching chapeau.

It takes a kid to look at you straight on like that, black sockets jumping out of frame.

If your under-painting were a cloudy globe, you too would color your lips red, groom your eyebrows, and hang your head.

Who doesn't think the rats should pay the Pied Piper, his instrument a broken flashlight, lovely curved rump one more hill they might seek to conquer?

The chimney smoke hasn't cooled the radioactive brain or warmed the dark windows.

It's only the seeing-eye rats and the courtiers who are in a hurry.

You could grow a face like the image of the earth as seen from space.

BRENDA COULTAS

AMERICAN CABINET

The trailer or double wide harbors dreams till the newness
is worn off. Metal door and steps lift up into a tornado sky.
On the walls, a portrait of a glowing cottage in the woods;
the chimney releases curly smoke. Inside is a ship in a
bottle or a trailer swimming in bottles. Shag and smoke,
recliners or originals.

Residents hear of murder, from far away to someone close
by. Crowbar in the living room. Attempted suicide in the
double wide next door after a doctor said "Wheelchair
within five years"

double wide despair to cathedral ceiling
packed high with papers
letters stacked, rubber banded and wedged
can't distinguish the valuables from the trash

cars stationary on blocks. Houses with taped fractured
windows.
hoarders in trailer park rags,
naked nearly, in our needs.

ALEX CUFF

THE TRIUMPH OF POVERTY

our banquet is in the sky. slice the moon into 1,672 even pieces.
one can't chew gold. everywhere a hand draping, wrapping,
steering skin of the past. the tree points where we should follow
her. smoke billows soot of insolent molecules: negligence and
memory. is that a bit in your mouth? we'd eat that chimney. if
it weren't in the background. a banquet of legs, an unenforced
migration for a new day. a rather disappointing gathering.

cross a rat with lemon grass stalk. that piece of sky so small.
weariness pressed beyond accumulated mud scars. put this in
your eye. west of heaven. to hold onto things isn't a new thing.
a profile is a thing that moves forward and a face one that binds.
string measures cranial perimeter. in this world, we form a
parallelogram. in this world, whose neckline is crossed.

STEVE DALACHINSKY

TOWN PICNIC

after the painting The Triumph of Poverty *by Nicole Eisenman with
a nod to Lucas Vostermann the Elder, after Hans Holbein the Younger*

"…you know I'd go from Rags to Riches"

1.

here too literal
pic / nic
where yer ass her - assed
he(arse) could easily be defaced
dimple in the domble fleurs
hat field's a real mc   coy
happy in our one-room country lack o'
                    liberties
   tiny infractions   hick up
gothic america's mis no mers
murmurs of in justice we stand
pointing our rewards in per suit of
                    novelties
shoes   t-shirt / cap
           guns
   how many bodies doth thou fit into a pick up ///?
                    Serve Up Vittles

2.

develop then
    they beat me up
these kids   kids kids
lyin in muck
dog / rain the bow wow
down pour heartbeat woof
of one   /   the other
    i like to be whole & pretty
        not a mess
nor retarded
                in case of fire follow
      the body
           heads up forward march backward
            toward
sprackle sky noonday's outing
        curvilinear landscape down there
            somewhere
     escaping the river's pull
       & behavioral management
          bed bugs no longer prioritize
    financial services   facial make overs
      relaxed as another knocked up madonna
      & chile

3.

  i look & things exist
  i think & only I exist
      masked by the color of race maps
                &
          Carrion   Crows
        images of poverty & wealth
              lost to us
        (w)hol(e)   bein(gs)
      sun holds history by a string
        holds grey night captive
        referencing former lives
    constant murder & mutilation by
              the elders
        thy body sinking into the muddy shit of...
    MODERATIO DILIGENTIA SOLICITUDO   NEGLIGENTIA
        PIGRITIA   ....IGNAVIA   MEMORIA
      INDUSTRIA   STUPIDITA....S
                LABOR
      IGNOBILEM   FALIBILEM INSTABILIS

for after all bankruptcy is not the end   it's a new beginning

4.
the green corners of earth
& flowers the colors of flags
what country does this buzzing in my ear belong to?
to whom does this suspicious vehicle belong?
a baseball card – buried beside a rotting branch
the entire forest up for sale
katydids all bastards since they never knew their parents

                    come to the gathering
activities include: food – drink – music – drugs – roller skates –
sack racing – double dutch – egg & spoon – leg relay – dancing
– dominoes – face painting – competition –
                              imprisonment

              bring the family   enjoy a day of fun!

The triumph of poverty eludes us. Mercy and art turn inward constricting at the throat. I imagine us surrounded by reality, not something outside, something like a patched quilt. The seasonal workers celebrating their temporary housing, the long view in someone's ear. And you, reading in your gray shirt, signing into the relentless sun.

JUDSON EVANS

TETANUS ARCH

after Nicole Eisenmen's Triumph of Poverty

Glue Bag Mom and Wire Hanger Dad stump
the P.T.A. arcade. Uncle Woodchuck and Aunt Hickory
dowse sentinels in ruin, call down crows
for their manna. Their ladder-in-moon child
Calamity Thyme smells of wet soap boxes.
The thread pulled through their tongues
teaches us to curb our appetite for flying colors,
to squander every crust. Gabbie Gangrene
wears auto parts on her head, a girdle of parking tickets,
certified letters. She fashions little flashlights
out of forceps. What happens inside the soup can is gossiped
on its label. Danny Darwin Jr. and Honest Abe Assassin screw asses
on backwards, strap glassware to collapsed porches.
Cousin Crawdad and Little Rich Girl never blink or spoil.
Ms. Mannerism suggests to Mandy Maelstrom
convenient places to store fat for lean times,
speak-easies for buying back her own breast milk.
Elevator Roy and Anaconda Floorboard don't respect the
yellow warning tape or Do Not Disturb signs around the seized
vehicles. The fisheye lenses grafted to their skin keep them cropped
and muffled while conducting tourists outside
the frame in garlands of poison sumac.

They offer beach bucket begging bowls filled with
coal tar. Jannisary J-Walk conducts a marathon
of sleepwalkers trying to distinguish lobes from fish hooks.
They only see themselves on Gas Station T.V., in the two-way
mirrors of manager trainees.

his top hat crumpled
his tie untied
his pants pulled down barely covering his knees
his buttocks where his genitals should be

the full moon shedding more light
than the puny flashlight in his right hand
ever possibly could

his left hand holding a string,
the other end of which
is tied around the pippilotti wrist of a
tiny fallen man
a man no bigger than the
rats that pass him by

several other tiny men,
the rats,
the crumpled top-hatted man,
a bloated boy,
a dog,
a woman holding a baby,
and several other multi-colored people
all walk in the same direction,

the same direction as a
fucked up, fucked up family
in a fucked up, fucked up old car

headed to nowhere?
to ruin?
or possibly just pacing,
back and forth,
all through the perfect night,
because where could they go,
under the beautiful full yellow moon,
the same yellow moon that shines on the
richest of the rich,
on people even poorer than these poor people,
and all of the rest of us?

EILEEN HENNESSY

HAPPY

the better days that are headed our way
(we're ready, we're waiting,
we're dressed in our best)

the land that bore up
the wheels of the car
that brought us to
the tree that stopped the car

the house that watches us waiting
(knock, and it shall be opened unto us)

the children learning to wait

the dog waiting for a bone
(he need only ask, and it shall be given to him)

the nightmares that fight for our feet

the tree the car the land
that watch us waiting

the days that are almost here
(see their light on our faces)

all of us, ready, dressed in our best
(top hat, tails, white silk shirt),

all of us, ready, waiting to greet
the better days that are surely headed our way

BONI JOI

IT WAS A FINE DAY FOR A PARADE

The sun was high
smoke from blue house with blue trim
and blackened windows
rushed out of a chimney on fire
the trees behind rich with leaves.

We were marching in the same direction
but we didn't look at each other.
Gathered around the car
ghosts of ancestors smashed in the backseat
some scarlet tourists stared ahead.

In the knee-high grass a pigment was led
by dislocated hand out of frame
the lady driving with the drunk nose
nuded it up to a fluke
and the Shakespearean puppets fooled around
in the mud poking each other with sticks
until they turned into a crowd of rats.

An olive green boy posed with a bowl like a statue
and next to him man in tux, holding a magazine light
pants down ass out and backwards
his dental floss strung one to of the actors

as he shined his light on the baby's mouth.

We couldn't tell what the dog was doing
he didn't belong to any of us
but he was cute.

CLAUDIA LA ROCCO

THE BETTER PART

You know, it's not for everybody, this continual living
The sun is a disaster
The colors are beautiful but, finally, none of the ladies can think
of anything else to say

They press her with endless invitations
She tries to stay in the house
Tries not to entertain carnal thoughts with regard to the gardener

(There is no gardener)
But the colors really are really, very, very beautiful

Somehow everything has been undone
The rabbit chases itself across the incessantly turning field
The trees show too much life

All this talk of living up to one's potential
There is something in this corner. Something devastating unfolds.
Her skin looks like shit

Everything comes from the word "remember"
You remember, don't you, she says, and it is not a question

Somewhere, surely, it is summertime still

And there is a moment for anything else

Discretion is the soul of valor, they told her when
she signed the papers
The state deregulates everything that can't be
bought and sold, she whispers back
The blue house is collapsing

We will always misunderstand each other:
Is that what living in the countryside is all about?
She wanted to get lost in a crowd not this crowd
but just some sort of terminal hanging around

The boy had drowned in the backyard
They fell over themselves to tell
Lost and found, it was in all the papers

There isn't anyone at the windows
He didn't, finally, make a sound
They appropriated her cause for their own designs

I am devoted to you, she whispered
She signed on the dotted line.

RONNA LEBO

WHAT IS WRONG WITH THEM

We've made it to the blind
outside of the house.

The chimney is on fire.
It looks like nice siding.

The German's rabbit won't start
so we'll walk under the piss moon.

We won't move formalism,
ass-led puppetry or rats past history.

Everyone knows it's all crime showbiz
or destiny appropriated without feeling.

We are closer than we think
to the deconstruction of our surrogate class.

Our patchwork nude steerage committee
leads melted cheese heroes.

Neglect-of-beauty passengers ride
away from home but there's no road
and we've all decided to go

one way to follow bloated Africa led
by the boney hand of Angelina Jolie.

Into our painted yard we launch
The Triumph Of Poverty.

JASON MARAK

EVERGREENS MOCK THE SEASONALLY STRICKEN—
THEY HAVE AND ALWAYS WILL

The problem is cyclical. Take,
for example, the sun
damage or retreads or primer-patched rust—
the blue trim, your skin, they peel
year after year after year. After
all, remember—chimney smoke only
means temporary heat and the need.
Someone will have to hear the cord
wood splitting all afternoon, again. It generates
a sucking thirst. So, we smoke
damage what we can. Water
damage the rest. And walk out
into the weak-mooned night, encouraged
not to cast even the smallest shadow.

The poor will always know how to party,
Despite poverty
And broken down cars
And front butts
Who've got you on a leash
Choking the will to live
Outta you
With too many Doritos
Too much crap beer
Dollar menu and snack foods
And diabetes
AIDS
Hep C
Hunger
And things you can't buy at
Whole Paycheck Foods
And no health insurance
Dental
Vacation
Or rest
With flat tires
Empty pockets
And cold nights
With the space heater

And overdue gas bill
Marked in bold red letters
Despite trying
Harder every day
The rich man's heaven
Is, in fact, the poor man's hell
But the rich man's heaven
Isn't so great
It's made of things
It's fake
Plastic and complacent
Built on others' suffering
The rich are just as miserable as the poor
And this is the triumph of poverty
The poor
Will inherit the earth
Will keep going
Because they're starved
Because they're ill
Because they've got nothing to lose
They'll keep trying to make a new world

While the rich have already given up.

ALBERT MOBILIO

TRIUMPH OF POVERTY

What did I expect when they said come now?
A road we'd be surrounded by?
Such strange flora, my pockets inside out.
Come rest your clothes while I rest mine.

What graph shows that we're slowly improving?
There's a newer model in the catalog.
We drive, carry, then drive some more.
Sky crowded with gray; its metal gone to smoke.

The decorations are dirty and the party's over.
Sleep on faces, faces hung like freight;
Eyes entertain an endless to-and-fro.
According to experts, heredity is our factor.

What's the story they tell about strangers at doors?
Zero times zero makes a scurrying sound.
Among monuments no one can bend.
What's usable gets used, the rest left out to rot.

YUKO OTOMO

THE TRIUMPH OF POVERTY

The difficulty in grasping
the details of an event

taking place
in a framed square space

did not make me feel
guilty for not being empathetic

toward the protagonists
who filled the empty landscape

inside it.
Allegorical expressions on their faces

told nothing but a collective silence
born out of some kind of inquisitive aggressiveness.

I felt good,
completely detached from them.

Poverty disguised as abundance
triumphed at their feet

where weeds grew

noiselessly.
Moon kept rising

as static attitudes of their language became
a part of nonchalant (un)Natural History.

HEALTH CARE

The nurses call him
Mr. Squats-to-Piss.
Waist surgically altered,
ass moved in front
to protect it and job,
though surely emeritus.

Escorted by secretary
turned mistress turned wife,
more disturbing
by showing up nude.
It's all she remembers
being good at.

He grabs the line's front,
mistakes alcohol smell
as coming from breaths
of poorly dressed,
calls for vice tests
before Medicare.

Wife scuttles behind,
demanding to know
who will check the scrotum.

Aides flock to deafness.
No-piece hiding rubber gloves,
she volunteers once more.

PHYLLIS ROSENZWEIG

LOVE MY NEED
(The Triumph of Poverty)

No break. I guess you saw this
the bluest sky today
intense green nests
some things with body parts
as sometimes a face
this painter
she had houses as heads
Sifting

Unplaced moments
talks, conversations and performances
positioned
errant histories
all created in white
The predicament of the human
A keener perception

Photographs of transcontinental migrating birds
of Caribou migrations
of The Last of The Mohicans
"'This is the apex' and 'here is the
relationship ...' and this ...
'this is the line of the orbit of the division'"

Neptune/Moon
This dismal category
"piglet pink"
where the nights are longest.

The quotes are from Jackson Pollock and T.J. Clark in
"The Unhappy Consciousness," in T.J. Clark, *Farewell to An Idea:
Episodes from a History of Modernism* (New Haven & London: Yale
University Press, 1999).

CATHERINE SHAINBERG

VOYEUR

The moon is blind and Brueghel's blind men are puppets now
In the junkyard full of the slow sound of northern faces
A dumb parade flaunts loud reds and rust
It is a droll still life celebrating the ages of man
Where mooning in top hat or parrot nosed, naked at the wheel
Is lost tense to the mud children and the ones behind the glass
No surface traction is to be had in the sands of mother love
The carcass of old bones frames a gymnast's inertia
Bare trees rise from bald skulls in a splendor of perforation
Whose fires rage in the shuttered house.

KAREN SHERMAN

DOWN THE CORNER

the demise of the world.

you shoved your hand into an enemy's pocket
to get back what was rightly yours,
though it was mine too

it was mine —
we argued about this all the time. each
little last flake of us that was left.
we were shared in the smallest parts and yet

always at odds, always the type who lived
for combat. we were so suited to each other,
so ass backwards we met cheek to cheek.
I'd walk around the block and bump into you again and again,
all lit up in our dull blaze.
the chevy novas burned overnight
the charred last signals from the tar fields.

I tossed everything I cared about into the bushes and ran.
the neighborhood took form behind me, rose up in a wall of
glittering debris
and then I never recognized anyone on the street anymore.
never ran into you anywhere.

you were having great success selling your belts, your
clothes, your stupid drawings.
everything of mine stayed on the blanket. always I had to
lug home the records, the figurines, the miniature ovens,
the carved mahogany chairs.
I didn't want to sit on them at home.
I didn't want.
I didn't.

I became someone on that corner – you know which
corner I mean.

and look
at us now.
asses turned back around, ambling through these
ridiculously open spaces,
knowing that everyone thinks we couldn't make it and
that we're invincible both.
you with your country life and me
nowhere.

in the middle of.

I'm the one
who's kept score

who bought your belts, your clothes, your drawings. your
oversized scissors.
your neighborhood fame, your pockmarks.
I have so much room here and still
they're hard to get at.
I can't manage the downtown pack, the cut and stacked.
they freeze and heat and freeze.
they fog the windows.
they blast out the doors.
rip every leaf from the trees

from the bushes.

ROBERT VANDERMOLEN

CICADAS IN JULY

The sheriff's deputy leaned on the open door
Of his cruiser, I never liked your name, he said

The man seated on a stump sighed—
Because of the light, the stream was salmon colored

A short wind coughed in a branch above his head

On a nearby estate the party had stalled
After margaritas. Lights flickered every so often

The actor, once famous for tense war roles,
Jumped on a sofa. I'm Captain America

He announced, waving his arms, bouncing
From cushion to cushion. Someone began to cry

Indeed, I was looking for Miss Terpstra
With her yellow dog Plato—she was my ride

Earlier on the veranda, the fields flowing down
From the knoll, looking like a postcard

From rural France

She had asked, what's in my hand?
I don't want to know, I replied

Walking back in leafy darkness, I pictured
A gentle tavern around a curve, past a glade

A sheriff's car sped past. Pebbles skittering.
Otherwise, tree frogs and crickets

Swallows and bats

I had a friend who was the only one left alive
When the enemy overran the perimeter

30 years later his therapist convinced him
He had been there, wounded

Lying in his bunker that night

*

Just when you believe matters are solved

*

I had a dream an Amish buggy rode up and slipped
Over the railing of the bridge

Cars stopped, fistfights ensued.
From the window of the motel I asked my son

Now how are we going to cross?

Then everyone on the bridge ran
As if fighters and bombers were approaching over water

Like what?
Like cartoon insects, small and large respectively

.

When I turned my son was also gone

ANNE WALDMAN

FORWARD & LUCID DREAM DAS CAPITAL

A being which does not have its nature outside
itself is not a natural being...
KARL MARX

you would say it you would paint it you would say it if you could

little rewards for the little people
the curb carbon people of the world...
primary people of the carbon litter world

they live the night
they live the night

little people of all our worlds & we them & they us

perpetually awake & facing forward. elegant. grotesque?
in all the trepidations of people people hear this now (oh people of
the world)

beautiful people of the world
dressed up worlds & wounds & weeds see the colors now

task them trouble them people people hear this now,
trouble this now, oh people of the world trouble trouble
& the children in the process coming to this edge & rhythmic

sadness

    curb carbon mantra
curb curb carbon carbon mantra

        mandate for the little people of the world
who rise in you strong and facing forward

exit the cars oh people of the world

cars of slick reticulated desire and abandon.

& shame shame shame shame to the people in the big house…

peregrination, migration, dust bowl & more masters

here go where did it go?
where go here did it go…

face forward, & again, masters again

tribe, a colony, an apex, a zero sum.

family, an exodus, a shift.

mask for the carnival and suit up here

face forward, & again, masters again

I hide in the spectacle of the state

an intergenerational institutional hidden apocalypse

a state of exception and torture

a chimerical party of hungry ghosts & danger zones
   where you could be held and hid (rise up rise up oh people of
the world)

how human and skewed are all rewards…

a small moon reticulated, and that is your word:
"a fine reticulation"

receding,

   chimney smoke you better see you better speak you better speak
you

all mean all mean you better rise

you would paint them
you
  w

ould
s   ee you wo

uld
rise

arise.

JOHN YAU

LOVE POEM

I was in love with you
which is why I walked

beside you
while you

drove a car
without doors

my pants crumpled
around my knees

It did not matter
that I was exposed

to the elements
the fire that fills each day

I was in love with you
and with the rats

swarming towards
the front of the line

I was in love with you
and the smoke

turning to gray goop
rising through leafy green trees

I was in love with you
and your porcine nose

the patches that held
your sawdust in

I rearranged my stovepipe hat
I wore the remnants of my last tuxedo

I walked beside the car
you drove down to the ground

Men in tunics
tumbled

beside their canes
I walked and walked

my pants crumpled
around my knees

Hold up the bowl
See what the moon

offers us tonight

CONTRIBUTORS

KOSTAS ANAGNOPOULOS is the founding editor of Insurance Editions, and his chapbooks include *Daydream, Irritant, Some of My Reasons* and *Various Sex Acts*. His first full-length collection, *Moving Blanket*, was published this year by Ugly Duckling Presse. Kostas was born and raised in Chicago, and he now lives in Queens, New York.

GALE BATCHELDER lives in Cambridge, Massachusetts. She has studied poetry in Provincetown, New York City, and Cambridge with Elizabeth Alexander, Gail Mazur, Tom Daley, and John Yau. Gale has been the featured reader at the Goba Salon, Text In-Between Poetry/Art series, and at Stone Soup Poetry. Her poetry has appeared in *White Whale Review*. An accomplished singer, Gale has recently served as President of the Mystic Chorale, a community chorus featuring world music. She received her BA in Philosophy and holds Master's degrees from Boston University and Harvard. Gale is the founder of New Leadership Group, a consulting firm serving nonprofit organizations world-wide.

BRENDA COULTAS has been a farmer, a carny, a taffy maker, a park ranger, a waitress in a disco ballroom, and the second woman welder in Firestone Steel's history. Her poetry has appeared in numerous publications, and she is the author of several books of poetry. Brenda lives in New York City.

ALEX CUFF was born in Brooklyn where she currently lives and teaches high school students. She is co-founder and co-editor of *No, Dear* magazine, a print journal featuring New York City poets. Her poetry and collage appear regularly in mailboxes all over the world.

STEVE DALACHINSKY was born in 1946, Brooklyn, New York. His work has appeared extensively in journals on & off line including; *Big Bridge, Milk, Unlikely Stories, Xpressed, Ratapallax, Evergreen Review, Long Shot, Alpha Beat Soup, Xtant, Blue Beat Jacket, N.Y. Arts Magazine, 88* and *Lost and Found Times*. He is included in such anthologies as *Beat Indeed, The Haiku Moment, Up is Up But So is Down: NYU Downtown Literary Anthology, the Unbearables* anthologies: *Help Yourself, The Worse Book I Ever Read* and the forthcoming *Big Book of Sex* (of which he is a co-editor) and the esteemed *Outlaw Bible of American Poetry*. He has written liner notes for the CDs of many artists including Anthony Braxton, Charles Gayle, James "Blood" Ulmer, Rashied Ali, Roy Campbell, Matthew Shipp and Roscoe Mitchell. His 1999 CD, *Incomplete Direction* (Knitting Factory Records), a collection of his poetry read in collaboration with various musicians, such as William Parker, Matthew Shipp, Daniel Carter, Sabir Mateen, Thurston Moore (Sonic Youth), Vernon Reid (Living Colour) has garnered much praise. His most recent chapbooks include *Musicology* (Editions Pioche, Paris 2005), *Trial and Error in Paris* (Loudmouth Collective 2003), Lautreamont's Laments (Furniture Press 2005), In *Glorious Black and White* (Ugly Duckling Presse 2005), *St. Lucie* (King of Mice Press 2005), *Are We Not* MEN & *Fake Book* (2 books of collage, 8 Page Press 2005), *Dream Book* (Avantcular Press 2005), *Christ Amongst the Fishes* (A book of collages, Oilcan Press 2009), *Insomnia Poems* (Propaganda Press 2009), *Invasion of the Animal People* (Propaganda Press 2010) and *the Mantis: the collected poems for Cecil Taylor 1966-2009* (Iniquity Press 2010). His books include *A Superintendent's Eyes* (Hozomeen Press 2000) and PEN Oakland National Book Award winning book *The Final Nite* (complete notes from a Charles Gayle Notebook, Ugly Duckling Presse 2006) and *Reaching into the Unknown* (A collaboration book project with photographer Jacques Bisceglia, Rogue Art 2009). His latest CD is *Phenomena of Interference,* a collaboration with pianist Matthew Shipp (Hopscotch Records 2005). He has read throughout the N.Y. area, the U.S., Japan and Europe, including France and Germany. He writes for *The Brooklyn Rail* as a contributing writer. He is active in the mail-art circuit & has shown his collages in Poets' Collages shows etc.

LYNNE DREYER was born in Baltimore, Maryland in 1950 and now lives in Falls Church, Virginia. She has been involved with the always changing but ever constant Washington D.C. poetry community for the last 28 years.

JUDSON EVANS is Director of Liberal Arts at The Boston Conservatory, where he teaches Ancient Greek culture and literature and a course on Utopian Communities. His work is represented in the third edition of Cor Van Den Heuvel's *The Haiku Anthology* (Norton 1999), in the first English language anthology of haibun, edited by Bruce Ross: *Journeys to the Interior* (Tuttle 1998) and in a chapbook *Mortal Coil,* from Leap Press. His poetic monologue *Scrabble Ridge* was staged as a performance piece by choreographer/dancer Julie Ince Thompson as part of the Fleet Boston Celebrity series in 2000. He was chosen as an "emerging poet" for the Association of American Poets by John Yau, and a selection of his poems with an essay on his work by John Yau appeared in *American Poet* in September of 2007.

JOHN S. HALL is the author of two books; *Jesus Was Way Cool* and *Daily Negations*, both published by Soft Skull Press, and he is the co-author of nine music CDs with his band, KING MISSILE, and he is also the co-author of one child.

EILEEN HENNESSY is a native of Long Island, and lives in New York City. Translator of foreign-language documentation, and adjunct associate professor of translation at New York University, her poems have been published in *Artful Dodge, Cream City Review, The Literary Review, Paris Review, Sanskrit,* and *Western Humanities Review.*

BONI JOI received an MFA in poetry from Columbia University, and has been nominated twice for a Pushcart Prize. Her poems have appeared in *Arbella, Boog City Reader, Long Shot, Lungfull, Ocular Press, Big Hammer, MaiNtENaNt3: a journal of contemporary dada writing & art* by Three Rooms Press, *The Brooklyn Rail* and many other journals. She has read her poetry at numerous venues in New York City and elsewhere.

CLAUDIA LA ROCCO writes about performance for the *New York Times* and is the founder of thePerformanceClub.org, which won a 2011 Arts Writers Grant. She is a member of Off The Park press, where she is currently editing an anthology of poems by painters. She is on the faculty of the School of Visual Art's graduate program in Art Criticism and Writing.

RONNA LEBO received an MFA from Mason Gross School of the Arts, and currently teaches at Kean University. She is the author of *Prolapse,* a book of prose poetry and sonnet-like work. She performed for twelve years as Alice B. Talkless, won a Jackie 60 New Artist Award, and was included in two CMJ music festivals. Her poetry has been published in *Ocular Press, Arbella, Long Shot, Big Hammer, Words, This Broken Shore, Whim Wit*, and the anthology *Will Work for Peace*, edited by Brett Axel.

JASON MARAK's work has appeared in *The Paris Review, Raritan,* and *Salmagundi*. He lives in Tokyo with his wife, the poet Jennifer Cahill, and their two children and teaches writing at Temple University's Japan campus.

REVEREND JEN MILLER is a performer, painter, playwright, Troll Museum Founder, underground movie star, open mike host, *Artnet* columnist, *ASS Magazine* founder and elf. Her books include *Live Nude Elf: the Sexperiments of Reverend Jen, Reverend Jen's Really Cool Neighborhood* and the upcoming *Elf Girl* (Simon & Schuster.) Her handcrafted art books can be found in collections including the Whitney Museum of American Art, the MoMA Library and the Warhol Museum.

YUKO OTOMO is of Japanese origin. A bilingual (Japanese & English) poet & a visual artist (in pursuit of Pure Abstraction). She also writes haiku, art criticism & essays. She has read in St. Mark's Poetry Project, Tribes, Bowery Poetry Club, ABC No Rio, La Mama, N.Y. Public Library, Knitting Factory, the Living Theatre, etc & in Japan, France & Germany. Her publication includes *Small Poems, The Hand of The Poet* (both from Ugly Duckling Presse) and *A Sunday Afternoon on the Isle of Museum* (Propaganda

Press) & *Fragile* (Sisyphus Press). She exhibited her art work at Courthouse Gallery at Anthology Film Archives & Vision Festival, etc.

CHAD PARENTEAU lives and works in the Boston area. He is the current host and organizer of the long-running Stone Soup Poetry series, recently creating its online extension, the journal *Spoonful*. His work has been published in *Shampoo, Main Street Rag, The November 3rd Club, Endicott Review, The Scrambler,* and the anthology *French Connections: A Gathering of Franco-American Poets.* His latest chapbook is *Discarded: Poems for My Apartments* from Cervená Barva Press.

PHYLLIS ROSENZWEIG lives in Washington, D.C. She has three chapbooks: *Seventeen Poems* (O Press, 1975), *Dogs* (Edge Books, 1996), and *Reasonable Accommodation* (Potes and Poets Press, 1997) and has more recently published in the *i.e. reader* (Baltimore: Narrow House Press, 2009) and *The Portable Boog Reader* (New York, 2010). From 1995 to 2008 she co-edited *Primary Writing* with Diane Ward.

CATHERINE SHAINBERG has an MFA in poetry from New York University. She founded The School of Images, a Kabbalah school to advance awareness of imagination as a tool for healing and creativity. Her book *Kabbalah and the Power of Dreaming* was published in 2005. Her next book *DreamBirth* is forthcoming. She has been published in *More Poems,* Alan Dugan's Poetry Workshops series, and Guggenheim Public. She has been a member of the writer's group, Off The Park, lead by John Yau, for the last seven years.

KAREN SHERMAN makes dances mostly, sometimes builds things, and writes also.

ROBERT VANDERMOLEN lives and works in Grand Rapids, Michigan. His most recent collection is *Water* (2009) with Michigan State University Press.

ANNE WALDMAN: Internationally recognized and acclaimed poet Anne Waldman has been an active member of the "Outrider" experimental poetry community, a culture she has helped create and nurture for over four decades as writer, editor, teacher, performer, magpie scholar, infra-structure curator and cultural/political activist. Her poetry is recognized in the lineage of Whitman and Ginsberg, and in the Beat, New York School and Black Mountain trajectories of the New American Poetry. She is the author of more than 40 books, including the mini-classic *Fast Speaking Woman*, a collection of essays entitled *Vow to Poetry* and several selected poems editions including *Helping the Dreamer, Kill or Cure* and *In the Room of Never Grieve*. She was one of the founders and directors of The Poetry Project at St. Mark's Church In-the-Bowery, working there for twelve years. She also co-founded with Allen Ginsberg the celebrated Jack Kerouac School of Disembodied Poetics at Naropa University, the first Buddhist inspired University in the western hemisphere, in 1974. Ginsberg has called Waldman his "spiritual wife." She is a Distinguished Professor of Poetics at Naropa and continues to work to preserve the school's substantial literary/oral archive. She has collaborated extensively with a number of artists, musicians, and dancers including George Schneeman, Elizabeth Murray, Richard

Tuttle, Donna Dennis and Pat Steir and the theatre director Judith Malina. Her play "Red Noir" was produced by the Living Theatre and ran for nearly three months in New York City in 2010. She has also been working most recently with other media including audio, film and video, with her husband, writer and video/film director Ed Bowes, and with her son, musician and composer Ambrose Bye. Waldman is a recipient of the Poetry Society of America's Shelley Memorial Award and has recently been appointed a Chancellor of The Academy of American Poets. *Manatee/Humanity* was published by Penguin Poets in 2009, and Waldman's next book *Gossamurmur* will be published by Penguin Poets in Spring of 2013. Her feminist epic *The Iovis Trllogy* received the 2012 PEN Center USA Award for Poetry. She divides her time between New York City and Boulder, Colorado. Her work has been translated into numerous languages.

JOHN YAU's recent publications include *Egyptian Sonnets* (Rain Taxi, 2012) and Further *Adventures in Monochrome* (Copper Canyon Press, 2012). He was the arts editor for *The Brooklyn Rail* (2007-2011). Since January 2012, his writing has appeared on Hyperallergic art blogazine. The founder and publisher of Black Square Editions, he teaches at Mason Gross School of the Arts (Rutgers University, the State University of New Jersey), and lives in New York.

OFF THE PARK PRESS warmly appreciates the following
people and organizations for their generousity
in furthering our publishing mission.

KIM FAMILY

SUSAN BERGER-JONES

THE ZANKEL FUND

NANCY ARONSON

NEW YORK COUNCIL OF
LITERARY MAGAZINES AND PRESSES

JOSEPH P. DONAHUE CHARITABLE
FOUNDATION TRUST

Five hundred copies of *The Triumph of Poverty* are
printed from Eric Gill's Joanna and Jean
Francois Porchez's Parisine Plus types.
The edition was printed & bound
by Thomson-Shore in
Dexter, Michigan.